MW00449900

Water Polo Team Notebook

Water Polo Team Notebook

Richard Kent and John Vargas

A companion book to

Writing on the Bus: Using Athletic Team Notebooks and Journals to Advance Learning and Performance in Sports

WritingAthletes.com

Dedication:

To Tyler, Ryan, and Victoria Kent, with love... *RK*

To my mom and dad, for a lifetime of love and support; and to my wife, my living angel... *JV*

Acknowledgements:

For contributions to this book, we thank Brian Avery, Rob Kent, Barbara Kalbus, Aaron Juarez, Susan Ortwein, Jonathan Barnea, Sheila Stawinski, Gayle Sirois, and members of the 2013 Stanford Men's Water Polo Team.

Copyright © 2014 Richard Kent
Writing Athletes
National Writing Project
All rights reserved.
ISBN-10: 0986019151

NATIONAL WRITING PROJECT

This book is published in cooperation with the National Writing Project, University of California, 2105 Bancroft Way, Berkeley, CA 94720

Contents

Introduction

"We write not to say what we know, but to learn, to discover, to know."
— Donald Murray, Pulitzer Prize Winner

For Players

The notebook you have in your hands can help you to become a better water polo player. By completing the book's activities, you will stay more organized and learn more about water polo and about yourself as a player. The ultimate purpose of this book is to help you become a *student of the game*.

The *Water Polo Team Notebook* will not replace good coaching or dedicated training. You're not going to instantaneously swim faster or score more goals because you wrote a Game Analysis or reflected on your play. But maintaining this notebook will make you a more knowledgeable athlete, and with that knowledge you will improve... and so will your team.

This notebook is a place to write about yourself as an athlete, teammate, and person while imagining your best. We challenge you to think deeply, to explore your understanding of the game of water polo, and to see yourself at the next level.

Protect your notebook in a zip-lock plastic bag and keep it in your athletic bag or locker. Carry a spare pen or pencil. You may end up sharing certain pages of your notebook with teammates and the coaching staff, so do your best to write legibly.

Finally, you should know that elite athletes like Olympians analyze their practice sessions and games in training logs, notebooks, and journals. Why is writing such a powerful way to learn? Author William Zinsser explains,

> "Writing organizes and clarifies our thoughts. Writing is how we think our way into a subject and make it our own. Writing enables us to find out what we know—and what we don't know—about whatever we're trying to learn."

Play well. Enjoy your teammates and the game of water polo.

For Coaches

As coaches, we never stop looking for ways to guide our players and teams to the next level. This book can complement your coaching practice, but only you can determine how.

Sport psychologists assign writing to help athletes look more closely at their training and competitions, and to work on issues like fear of failure. They understand that writing can affect an athlete's physical and emotional well-being by reducing stress and anxiety, increasing self-awareness, sharpening mental skills, and strengthening coping abilities. Writing also complements other psychological techniques like meditation and visualization.

Throughout the *Water Polo Team Notebook*, your athletes (and you, if you choose to write) will analyze, process, and reflect on practices, games, and life in and out of the pool. There are countless ways to use the sections of this notebook. Here's one example:

After a game have your players complete a Game Analysis I. At the next practice, ask players to divide up into small groups and discuss their analyses for a few minutes. Then, bring the small groups together for a full team discussion of each group's observations. The same activity can be done with other sections of the book. Small and large group discussions give most players an opportunity to talk, share ideas, and learn.

If you collect notebooks to review during the season, you may want to jot notes to your players in "Coach's Comments" at the back of the book. But, that's totally up to you. We do know that you'll learn more about your players—and your team—by reading the notebooks at some point during the season.

There are many ways to learn as an athlete; writing is one of them. "We write not to say what we know," said Pulitzer Prize winner Donald Murray, "but to learn, to discover, to know." This is to say that writing is a powerful way to learn, and that's why scientists, historians, and athletes keep notebooks, logs, and journals.

Finally, we suggest that you read *Writing on the Bus: Using Athletic Team Notebooks and Journals to Advance Learning and Performance in Sports* (2012). This book offers practical examples for using team notebooks and presents the theories that support the use of writing as way to learn in athletics.

We also invite you to check out our resource website at WritingAthletes.com. Very best wishes to you and your team.

Richard Kent   John Vargas
Orono, Maine   *Stanford, California*

Preseason Thoughts

"We are what we repeatedly do. Excellence, therefore, is not an act, but a habit."

—Aristotle

Preseason Thoughts

What were your strengths last season as a water polo player? When asked to name strengths some players said that they were...

Focused   *Dedicated*   *Strong*   *Disciplined*   *Responsible*   *Skillful*
Confident   *Competitive*   *Motivated*   *Courageous*   *Positive*   *Fit*

List your strengths and write about one:

Last season, in what areas did your playing skills need to improve?

In the offseason, what did you do to improve as a water polo player?

Describe your most satisfying performance last season during a match or a training session. What contributed to this performance?

Describe your most disappointing performance from last season. What contributed to this performance?

What are your Personal Athletic Goals for this season? A personal goal is not "I'm going to score 7 goals this season." A personal goal is a specific performance objective you plan to accomplish. Perhaps you plan to improve your shots for accuracy or strengthen your legs:

Personal Athletic Goals	What will you do to reach your Personal Athletic Goals?	Who might help you reach these goals?
–Improve my leg strength.	–I will spend 10 minutes after practice each day and do extra leg work.	–I will pick a different teammate each practice to stay and work with me.

Personal Athletic Goals	What will you do to reach your Personal Athletic Goals?	Who might help you reach these goals?
1.	1.	1.
2.	2.	2.
3.	3.	3.

Last year our team strengths included the following:

Last year our team needed to work more in the following areas:

Describe the most satisfying team performance last season during a match or a training session. What contributed to this performance?

Describe the most disappointing team performance from last season. What contributed to this performance?

What do you believe this year's team strengths will be?

In what areas will this year's team need to improve?

Final thoughts on the upcoming season:

Notes

Midseason Thoughts

Midseason Thoughts

What are your strengths so far this season as a water polo player?

In what areas do you need to improve?

What's your most significant out-of-the-pool accomplishment so far this season? (e.g., nutrition, grades, proper sleep, time management)

Write about your best personal performance so far this season. What contributed to your success?

Write about your worst performance so far this season. What contributed to your poor play? How did you rebound from that performance?

So far this season our team strengths include...

Our team needs to improve in the following areas...

Personal Athletic Goals

Go back to the three Personal Athletic Goals that you established at the beginning of this workbook. List them below. Rank your effectiveness in each on the numeric chart.

Goal 1: _____

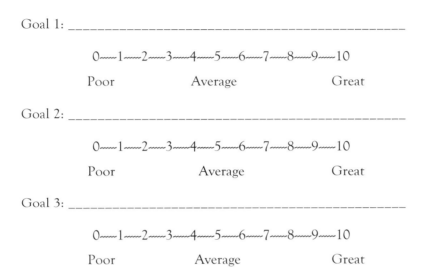

0——1——2——3——4——5——6——7——8——9——10

Poor   Average   Great

Goal 2: _____

0——1——2——3——4——5——6——7——8——9——10

Poor   Average   Great

Goal 3: _____

0——1——2——3——4——5——6——7——8——9——10

Poor   Average   Great

What specific work or activities are you doing to pursue these goals?

If you believe you are being successful in pursuing these goals, how do you know this? What evidence is there?

Midseason Thoughts

Write about your overall performance thus far and how you will continue to improve <u>and</u> serve the team.

Postseason Thoughts

"In the end, it's extra effort that separates a winner from second place. But winning takes a lot more than that, too. It starts with complete command of the fundamentals. Then it takes desire, determination, discipline, and self-sacrifice. And, finally, it takes a great deal of love, fairness and respect for your fellow man. Put all these together, and even if you don't win, how can you lose?"

–Jesse Owens

Postseason Thoughts

What have been your strengths this season as a water polo player?

What areas still need improvement?

What has been your most significant out-of-the-pool accomplishment this season? (e.g., nutrition, grades, proper sleep, time management)

Write about your best personal performance this season in a game or practice session. What contributed to your success?

Write about your worst performance this season in a game or practice session. What contributed to this performance? How did you rebound from that performance?

This season our team strengths included...

Our team still needed to work on the following areas...

What are your plans in the offseason for training?

Go back to the three Personal Athletic Goals that you established at the beginning of this workbook. List and rank your effectiveness below.

Goal 1: _____

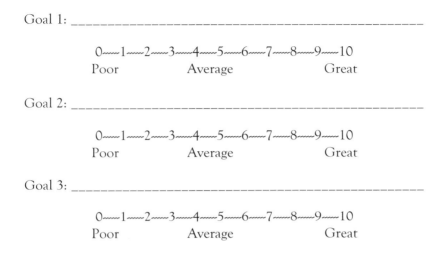

0~~1~~2~~3~~4~~5~~6~~7~~8~~9~~10
Poor   Average   Great

Goal 2: _____

0~~1~~2~~3~~4~~5~~6~~7~~8~~9~~10
Poor   Average   Great

Goal 3: _____

0~~1~~2~~3~~4~~5~~6~~7~~8~~9~~10
Poor   Average   Great

What did you do to be successful in pursuing these goals?

If you were successful, how do you know this? What evidence is there?

In what areas do you need to improve to achieve any of these goals in the future?

Game Analysis I

Instructions for *Game Analysis I*

The prompts on these pages provide you with an opportunity to analyze your game. Unpacking a water polo game in this fashion, whether you were a substitute or played every minute, helps you think more objectively while seeing the larger picture of a game. This thinking will help you improve your understanding of water polo. The *GAI* may be used for scrimmages and intrasquad games as well as your league or conference games.

When you fill out a *GAI*, don't be overly concerned about the conventions of writing. In other words, don't worry about spelling, grammar, and paragraphing... *just write.*

Checkout the model *GAI* on the next page and look closely at the way the player addressed certain prompts. But remember, these are just models—you'll have your own way of telling the story of a game.

In the final section of the *GAI*, you'll see a Player Check-in. This section can usually be accomplished quickly. Don't sit around and ponder life. Give a general response that reflects your immediate thought. Rate each topic in the Player Check-in using the following scale:

Above Average (+)   Average (O)   Below Average (−)

As you go through these topics, focus on the following:

<u>Health:</u>	How's my over all health?
<u>Sleep:</u>	Am I getting enough sleep each night?
<u>Hydration:</u>	Do I take in enough water throughout the day as well as before, during, and after a game?
<u>Fitness:</u>	How's my overall fitness level?
<u>Nutrition:</u>	The USDA has a basic informational Website that offers nutritional guidance about the consumption of food (see ChooseMyPlate.Gov). For purposes of the Player Check-in, ask yourself whether you've eaten the suggested foods of a healthy diet (i.e., grains, proteins, veggies, fruit).

If you have further questions about the *GAI*, ask your coach. If you have questions, you can bet several of your teammates do, too.

-MODEL-

 *Game Analysis I*

Opponent: <u>UCLA</u> (Wins <u>12</u> Losses <u>0</u>)   Date: <u>11/13</u>   Result: <u>10-5 Loss</u>

Location: <u>UCI</u> Stanford Record: Wins: <u>10</u> Losses: <u>2</u> Minutes Played: <u>20+-</u>

- My strengths as a player in today's game:
    - *Drew 4 ejections*
    - *Drew 1 offensive*
    - *Held a side for majority (Note: not always deep enough)*
    - *Responded relatively well to abnormal amount of playing time against quality opponent*

- My weaknesses as a player in today's game:
    - *Was countered on "several" occasions*
    - *Wasn't set deep enough to allow shooters a better angle*
    - *Was extremely gassed on multiple occasions*
    - *5 man defense*
    - *Snapping to ball and getting off a quality shot*
    - *Keeping my head up at set*

- Team strengths (e.g., defense, offense, 5 v 6, 6 v 5) in today's game:
    - *Overall resiliency (after going down something like 7-1)*
    - *2nd Team performance (more minutes than usual)*

- Team weaknesses in today's game:
    - *Shooting*
    - *5-man defense*
    - *Finishing plays*

- Opponent's team strengths:
    - *Consistent pressure*
    - *Good 6-5 percentage*

- Opponent's team weaknesses:
    - *Complacent in the last quarter*

- What was the "difference" in today's game:
    - *We were unable to find ways to score and finish plays*
    - *The team that better capitalized on the other team's mistakes won*
    - *UCLA scored on opportunities they should have scored while we didn't*
    - *Fitness could have been factor... we just came off playing a physical game vs. Cal*

- What team adjustment would you suggest for the next game against this opponent?
    - *Come out with an attack mentality*
    - *Finish plays on 6-5 and counterattack*

- Who was the Player of the Game and why?
    - *For Stanford – Goalkeeper – Even though the game quickly got away from us, he showed maturity in his continued aggression and attack. Clearly displayed his will to win even when against the wall.*
    - *For UCLA – Goalie/5 man defense – We maybe scored 1 of 12 man-ups. That's either a terrible performance by us or great defense by them.*

- Other comments (e.g., team strategy, attitude, preparation....)
    - *Having the 4-5 seed presented a mental challenge for our team especially going into the second day of the tournament. We played 3 quality teams over the weekend and this game was a lapse of focus and attack. Since our team relies so heavily on the play of our starters, the physical task of playing 3 tough games really begins to show come the last two games. Whether or not our squad coming off the bench can play quality minutes and give them a break dictates a lot of our success.*

Player Check-in

Above Average (+)   Average (O)   Below Average (–)

Health	O	Nutrition: Grains	O
Sleep	O	Protein	+
Hydration	O	Veggies	+
Fitness	O	Fruit	O

Life Beyond Water Polo O

Quotable Quote: Coach's favorite line: "Think and play with discipline."

Game Analysis I

Opponent: _____(Wins ___ Losses ___) Date: ____ Result:____

Location: ____ Record: Wins: ___ Losses: ___ Minutes Played: ____

- My strengths as a player in today's game:

- My weaknesses as a player in today's game:

- Team strengths (e.g., defense, offense, 5 v 6, 6 v 5) in today's game:

- Team weaknesses in today's game:

- Opponent's team strengths:

- Opponent's team weaknesses:

– What was the "difference" in today's match:

– What team adjustment would you suggest for the next game against this opponent?

– Who was the Player of the Game and why?

– Other comments (e.g., team strategy, attitude, preparation....)

Player Check-in
Above Average (+)   Average (O)   Below Average (–)

Health   ____   *Nutrition:* Grains ____

Sleep   ____   Protein ____

Hydration ____   Veggies ____

Fitness   ____   Fruit   ____

Life Beyond Water Polo ____

Quotable Quote: _____

_____

Game Analysis I

Opponent: _____(Wins ___ Losses ___) Date: ____ Result:____

Location: ____ Record: Wins: ___ Losses: ___ Minutes Played: ____

– My strengths as a player in today's game:

– My weaknesses as a player in today's game:

– Team strengths (e.g., defense, offense, 5 v 6, 6 v 5) in today's game:

– Team weaknesses in today's game:

– Opponent's team strengths:

– Opponent's team weaknesses:

– What was the "difference" in today's match:

– What team adjustment would you suggest for the next game against this opponent?

– Who was the Player of the Game and why?

– Other comments (e.g., team strategy, attitude, preparation....)

Player Check-in
Above Average (+) Average (O) Below Average (–)

Health   ____   *Nutrition:* Grains ____

Sleep   ____   Protein ____

Hydration ____   Veggies ____

Fitness   ____   Fruit   ____

Life Beyond Water Polo ____

Quotable Quote: _____

_____

 *Game Analysis I*

Opponent: _____(Wins ___ Losses ___) Date: ____ Result:____

Location: ____ Record: Wins: ___ Losses: ___ Minutes Played: ____

- My strengths as a player in today's game:

- My weaknesses as a player in today's game:

- Team strengths (e.g., defense, offense, 5 v 6, 6 v 5) in today's game:

- Team weaknesses in today's game:

- Opponent's team strengths:

- Opponent's team weaknesses:

– What was the "difference" in today's match:

– What team adjustment would you suggest for the next game against this opponent?

– Who was the Player of the Game and why?

– Other comments (e.g., team strategy, attitude, preparation....)

Player Check-in
Above Average (+)   Average (O)   Below Average (–)

Health   ____   *Nutrition:* Grains ____

Sleep   ____   Protein ____

Hydration ____   Veggies ____

Fitness   ____   Fruit   ____

Life Beyond Water Polo ____

Quotable Quote: _____

_____

Game Analysis I

Opponent: _____(Wins ___ Losses ___) Date: ____ Result:____

Location: ____ Record: Wins: ___ Losses: ___ Minutes Played: ____

- My strengths as a player in today's game:

- My weaknesses as a player in today's game:

- Team strengths (e.g., defense, offense, 5 v 6, 6 v 5) in today's game:

- Team weaknesses in today's game:

- Opponent's team strengths:

- Opponent's team weaknesses:

-   What was the "difference" in today's match:

-   What team adjustment would you suggest for the next game against this opponent?

-   Who was the Player of the Game and why?

-   Other comments (e.g., team strategy, attitude, preparation....)

Player Check-in

Above Average (+)   Average (O)   Below Average (–)

Health   ____   *Nutrition:* Grains ____

Sleep   ____   Protein ____

Hydration ____   Veggies ____

Fitness   ____   Fruit   ____

Life Beyond Water Polo ____

Quotable Quote: _____

_____

____

Game Analysis I

Opponent: _____(Wins ___ Losses ___) Date: ____ Result:____

Location: ____ Record: Wins: ___ Losses: ___ Minutes Played: ____

– My strengths as a player in today's game:

– My weaknesses as a player in today's game:

– Team strengths (e.g., defense, offense, 5 v 6, 6 v 5) in today's game:

– Team weaknesses in today's game:

– Opponent's team strengths:

– Opponent's team weaknesses:

– What was the "difference" in today's match:

– What team adjustment would you suggest for the next game against this opponent?

– Who was the Player of the Game and why?

– Other comments (e.g., team strategy, attitude, preparation....)

Player Check-in
Above Average (+)   Average (O)   Below Average (–)

Health	____	Nutrition: Grains	____
Sleep	____	Protein	____
Hydration	____	Veggies	____
Fitness	____	Fruit	____

Life Beyond Water Polo ____

Quotable Quote: _____

_____

 *Game Analysis I*

Opponent: _____(Wins ___ Losses ___) Date: ____ Result:____

Location: ____ Record: Wins: ___ Losses: ___ Minutes Played: ____

- My strengths as a player in today's game:

- My weaknesses as a player in today's game:

- Team strengths (e.g., defense, offense, 5 v 6, 6 v 5) in today's game:

- Team weaknesses in today's game:

- Opponent's team strengths:

- Opponent's team weaknesses:

– What was the "difference" in today's match:

– What team adjustment would you suggest for the next game against this opponent?

– Who was the Player of the Game and why?

– Other comments (e.g., team strategy, attitude, preparation....)

Player Check-in
Above Average (+)   Average (O)   Below Average (–)

Health   ____

Sleep   ____

Hydration ____

Fitness   ____

Nutrition: Grains ____

Protein ____

Veggies ____

Fruit   ____

Life Beyond Water Polo ____

Quotable Quote: _____

_____

Game Analysis I

Opponent: _____(Wins ___ Losses ___) Date: ____ Result:____

Location: ____ Record: Wins: ___ Losses: ___ Minutes Played: ____

– My strengths as a player in today's game:

– My weaknesses as a player in today's game:

– Team strengths (e.g., defense, offense, 5 v 6, 6 v 5) in today's game:

– Team weaknesses in today's game:

– Opponent's team strengths:

– Opponent's team weaknesses:

- What was the "difference" in today's match:

- What team adjustment would you suggest for the next game against this opponent?

- Who was the Player of the Game and why?

- Other comments (e.g., team strategy, attitude, preparation....)

Player Check-in
Above Average (+)   Average (O)   Below Average (–)

Health ____		Nutrition: Grains ____
Sleep ____		Protein ____
Hydration ____		Veggies ____
Fitness ____		Fruit ____

Life Beyond Water Polo ____

Quotable Quote: _____

_____

____

Game Analysis I

Opponent: _____(Wins ___ Losses ___) Date: ____ Result:____

Location: ____ Record: Wins: ___ Losses: ___ Minutes Played: ____

- My strengths as a player in today's game:

- My weaknesses as a player in today's game:

- Team strengths (e.g., defense, offense, 5 v 6, 6 v 5) in today's game:

- Team weaknesses in today's game:

- Opponent's team strengths:

- Opponent's team weaknesses:

– What was the "difference" in today's match:

– What team adjustment would you suggest for the next game against this opponent?

– Who was the Player of the Game and why?

– Other comments (e.g., team strategy, attitude, preparation....)

Player Check-in
Above Average (+)   Average (O)   Below Average (–)

Health   ____   *Nutrition:* Grains ____

Sleep   ____   Protein ____

Hydration ____   Veggies ____

Fitness   ____   Fruit   ____

Life Beyond Water Polo ____

Quotable Quote: _____

_____

Game Analysis I

Opponent: _____(Wins ___ Losses ___) Date: ____ Result:____

Location: ____ Record: Wins: ___ Losses: ___ Minutes Played: ____

- My strengths as a player in today's game:

- My weaknesses as a player in today's game:

- Team strengths (e.g., defense, offense, 5 v 6, 6 v 5) in today's game:

- Team weaknesses in today's game:

- Opponent's team strengths:

- Opponent's team weaknesses:

–   What was the "difference" in today's match:

–   What team adjustment would you suggest for the next game against this opponent?

–   Who was the Player of the Game and why?

–   Other comments (e.g., team strategy, attitude, preparation....)

Player Check-in
Above Average (+)   Average (O)   Below Average (–)

Health   ____   *Nutrition:* Grains ____

Sleep   ____   Protein ____

Hydration ____   Veggies ____

Fitness   ____   Fruit   ____

Life Beyond Water Polo ____

Quotable Quote: _____

_____

Game Analysis I

Opponent: _____(Wins ___ Losses ___) Date: ____ Result:____

Location: ____ Record: Wins: ___ Losses: ___ Minutes Played: ____

- My strengths as a player in today's game:

- My weaknesses as a player in today's game:

- Team strengths (e.g., defense, offense, 5 v 6, 6 v 5) in today's game:

- Team weaknesses in today's game:

- Opponent's team strengths:

- Opponent's team weaknesses:

–   What was the "difference" in today's match:

–   What team adjustment would you suggest for the next game against this opponent?

–   Who was the Player of the Game and why?

–   Other comments (e.g., team strategy, attitude, preparation....)

Player Check-in
Above Average (+)   Average (O)   Below Average (–)

Health   ____   *Nutrition:* Grains ____

Sleep   ____   Protein ____

Hydration ____   Veggies ____

Fitness   ____   Fruit   ____

Life Beyond Water Polo ____

Quotable Quote: _____

_____

 *Game Analysis I*

Opponent: _____(Wins ___ Losses ___) Date: ____ Result:____

Location: ____ Record: Wins: ___ Losses: ___ Minutes Played: ____

- My strengths as a player in today's game:

- My weaknesses as a player in today's game:

- Team strengths (e.g., defense, offense, 5 v 6, 6 v 5) in today's game:

- Team weaknesses in today's game:

- Opponent's team strengths:

- Opponent's team weaknesses:

–   What was the "difference" in today's match:

–   What team adjustment would you suggest for the next game against this opponent?

–   Who was the Player of the Game and why?

–   Other comments (e.g., team strategy, attitude, preparation....)

Player Check-in
Above Average (+)   Average (O)   Below Average (–)

Health   ____

Sleep   ____

Hydration ____

Fitness   ____

Nutrition: Grains ____

Protein ____

Veggies ____

Fruit   ____

Life Beyond Water Polo ____

Quotable Quote: _____

_____

Game Analysis I

Opponent: _____(Wins ___ Losses ___) Date: ____ Result:____

Location: ____ Record: Wins: ___ Losses: ___ Minutes Played: ____

- My strengths as a player in today's game:

- My weaknesses as a player in today's game:

- Team strengths (e.g., defense, offense, 5 v 6, 6 v 5) in today's game:

- Team weaknesses in today's game:

- Opponent's team strengths:

- Opponent's team weaknesses:

– What was the "difference" in today's match:

– What team adjustment would you suggest for the next game against this opponent?

– Who was the Player of the Game and why?

– Other comments (e.g., team strategy, attitude, preparation....)

Player Check-in
Above Average (+)   Average (O)   Below Average (–)

Health ____   Nutrition: Grains ____

Sleep ____   Protein ____

Hydration ____   Veggies ____

Fitness ____   Fruit ____

Life Beyond Water Polo ____

Quotable Quote: _____

_____

 *Game Analysis I*

Opponent: _____(Wins ___ Losses ___) Date: ____ Result:____

Location: ____ Record: Wins: ___ Losses: ___ Minutes Played: ____

- My strengths as a player in today's game:

- My weaknesses as a player in today's game:

- Team strengths (e.g., defense, offense, 5 v 6, 6 v 5) in today's game:

- Team weaknesses in today's game:

- Opponent's team strengths:

- Opponent's team weaknesses:

–   What was the "difference" in today's match:

–   What team adjustment would you suggest for the next game against this opponent?

–   Who was the Player of the Game and why?

–   Other comments (e.g., team strategy, attitude, preparation....)

Player Check-in
Above Average (+)   Average (O)   Below Average (–)

Health   ____

Sleep   ____

Hydration ____

Fitness   ____

Nutrition: Grains ____

Protein ____

Veggies ____

Fruit   ____

Life Beyond Water Polo ____

Quotable Quote: _____

_____

 *Game Analysis I*

Opponent: _____(Wins ___ Losses ___) Date: ____ Result:____

Location: ____ Record: Wins: ___ Losses: ___ Minutes Played: ____

- My strengths as a player in today's game:

- My weaknesses as a player in today's game:

- Team strengths (e.g., defense, offense, 5 v 6, 6 v 5) in today's game:

- Team weaknesses in today's game:

- Opponent's team strengths:

- Opponent's team weaknesses:

– What was the "difference" in today's match:

– What team adjustment would you suggest for the next game against this opponent?

– Who was the Player of the Game and why?

– Other comments (e.g., team strategy, attitude, preparation....)

Player Check-in
Above Average (+)   Average (O)   Below Average (–)

Health   ____   *Nutrition:* Grains ____

Sleep   ____   Protein ____

Hydration ____   Veggies ____

Fitness   ____   Fruit   ____

Life Beyond Water Polo ____

Quotable Quote: _____

_____

Game Analysis I

Opponent: _____(Wins ___ Losses ___) Date: ____   Result:____

Location: ____   Record: Wins: ___ Losses: ___ Minutes Played: ____

-   My strengths as a player in today's game:

-   My weaknesses as a player in today's game:

-   Team strengths (e.g., defense, offense, 5 v 6, 6 v 5) in today's game:

-   Team weaknesses in today's game:

-   Opponent's team strengths:

-   Opponent's team weaknesses:

– What was the "difference" in today's match:

– What team adjustment would you suggest for the next game against this opponent?

– Who was the Player of the Game and why?

– Other comments (e.g., team strategy, attitude, preparation....)

Player Check-in

Above Average (+)   Average (O)   Below Average (–)

Health   ____   *Nutrition:* Grains ____

Sleep   ____   Protein ____

Hydration ____   Veggies ____

Fitness   ____   Fruit   ____

Life Beyond Water Polo ____

Quotable Quote: _____

_____

 *Game Analysis I*

Opponent: _____(Wins ___ Losses ___) Date: ____ Result:____

Location: ____ Record: Wins: ___ Losses: ___ Minutes Played: ____

– My strengths as a player in today's game:

– My weaknesses as a player in today's game:

– Team strengths (e.g., defense, offense, 5 v 6, 6 v 5) in today's game:

– Team weaknesses in today's game:

– Opponent's team strengths:

– Opponent's team weaknesses:

– What was the "difference" in today's match:

– What team adjustment would you suggest for the next game against this opponent?

– Who was the Player of the Game and why?

– Other comments (e.g., team strategy, attitude, preparation....)

Player Check-in
Above Average (+)   Average (O)   Below Average (–)

Health ____		*Nutrition:* Grains ____
Sleep ____		Protein ____
Hydration ____		Veggies ____
Fitness ____		Fruit ____

Life Beyond Water Polo ____

Quotable Quote: _____

_____

Game Analysis I

Opponent: _____(Wins ___ Losses ___) Date: ____ Result:____

Location: ____ Record: Wins: ___ Losses: ___ Minutes Played: ____

– My strengths as a player in today's game:

– My weaknesses as a player in today's game:

– Team strengths (e.g., defense, offense, 5 v 6, 6 v 5) in today's game:

– Team weaknesses in today's game:

– Opponent's team strengths:

– Opponent's team weaknesses:

– What was the "difference" in today's match:

– What team adjustment would you suggest for the next game against this opponent?

– Who was the Player of the Game and why?

– Other comments (e.g., team strategy, attitude, preparation....)

Player Check-in
Above Average (+)   Average (O)   Below Average (–)

Health   ____   *Nutrition:* Grains ____

Sleep   ____   Protein ____

Hydration ____   Veggies ____

Fitness   ____   Fruit   ____

Life Beyond Water Polo ____

Quotable Quote: _____

_____

Game Analysis I

Opponent: _____(Wins ___ Losses ___) Date: ____ Result:____

Location: ____ Record: Wins: ___ Losses: ___ Minutes Played: ____

- My strengths as a player in today's game:

- My weaknesses as a player in today's game:

- Team strengths (e.g., defense, offense, 5 v 6, 6 v 5) in today's game:

- Team weaknesses in today's game:

- Opponent's team strengths:

- Opponent's team weaknesses:

–   What was the "difference" in today's match:

–   What team adjustment would you suggest for the next game against this opponent?

–   Who was the Player of the Game and why?

–   Other comments (e.g., team strategy, attitude, preparation....)

Player Check-in

Above Average (+)   Average (O)   Below Average (–)

Health   ____   *Nutrition:* Grains ____

Sleep   ____   Protein ____

Hydration ____   Veggies ____

Fitness   ____   Fruit   ____

Life Beyond Water Polo ____

Quotable Quote: _____

_____

Game Analysis I

Opponent: _____(Wins ___ Losses ___) Date: ____ Result:____

Location: ____ Record: Wins: ___ Losses: ___ Minutes Played: ____

–   My strengths as a player in today's game:

–   My weaknesses as a player in today's game:

–   Team strengths (e.g., defense, offense, 5 v 6, 6 v 5) in today's game:

–   Team weaknesses in today's game:

–   Opponent's team strengths:

–   Opponent's team weaknesses:

– What was the "difference" in today's match:

– What team adjustment would you suggest for the next game against this opponent?

– Who was the Player of the Game and why?

– Other comments (e.g., team strategy, attitude, preparation....)

Player Check-in
Above Average (+)   Average (O)   Below Average (–)

Health   ____   *Nutrition:* Grains ____

Sleep   ____   Protein ____

Hydration ____   Veggies ____

Fitness   ____   Fruit   ____

Life Beyond Water Polo ____

Quotable Quote: _____

_____

Game Analysis I

Opponent: _____(Wins ___ Losses ___) Date: ____ Result:____

Location: ____ Record: Wins: ___ Losses: ___ Minutes Played: ____

– My strengths as a player in today's game:

– My weaknesses as a player in today's game:

– Team strengths (e.g., defense, offense, 5 v 6, 6 v 5) in today's game:

– Team weaknesses in today's game:

– Opponent's team strengths:

– Opponent's team weaknesses:

– What was the "difference" in today's match:

– What team adjustment would you suggest for the next game against this opponent?

– Who was the Player of the Game and why?

– Other comments (e.g., team strategy, attitude, preparation....)

Player Check-in
Above Average (+)   Average (O)   Below Average (–)

Health   ____

Sleep   ____

Hydration ____

Fitness   ____

Nutrition: Grains ____

Protein ____

Veggies ____

Fruit   ____

Life Beyond Water Polo ____

Quotable Quote: _____

_____

Game Analysis I

Opponent: _____(Wins ___ Losses ___) Date: ____ Result:____

Location: ____ Record: Wins: ___ Losses: ___ Minutes Played: ____

–   My strengths as a player in today's game:

–   My weaknesses as a player in today's game:

–   Team strengths (e.g., defense, offense, 5 v 6, 6 v 5) in today's game:

–   Team weaknesses in today's game:

–   Opponent's team strengths:

–   Opponent's team weaknesses:

– What was the "difference" in today's match:

– What team adjustment would you suggest for the next game against this opponent?

– Who was the Player of the Game and why?

– Other comments (e.g., team strategy, attitude, preparation....)

Player Check-in
Above Average (+)   Average (O)   Below Average (–)

Health   ____   *Nutrition:* Grains ____

Sleep   ____   Protein ____

Hydration ____   Veggies ____

Fitness   ____   Fruit   ____

Life Beyond Water Polo ____

Quotable Quote: _____

_____

Game Analysis I

Opponent: _____(Wins ___ Losses ___) Date: ____ Result:____

Location: ____ Record: Wins: ___ Losses: ___ Minutes Played: ____

-   My strengths as a player in today's game:

-   My weaknesses as a player in today's game:

-   Team strengths (e.g., defense, offense, 5 v 6, 6 v 5) in today's game:

-   Team weaknesses in today's game:

-   Opponent's team strengths:

-   Opponent's team weaknesses:

- What was the "difference" in today's match:

- What team adjustment would you suggest for the next game against this opponent?

- Who was the Player of the Game and why?

- Other comments (e.g., team strategy, attitude, preparation....)

Player Check-in
Above Average (+)   Average (O)   Below Average (–)

Health   ____

Sleep   ____

Hydration ____

Fitness   ____

Nutrition: Grains ____

Protein ____

Veggies ____

Fruit   ____

Life Beyond Water Polo ____

Quotable Quote: _____

_____

Game Analysis I

Opponent: _____(Wins ___ Losses ___) Date: ____ Result:____

Location: ____ Record: Wins: ___ Losses: ___ Minutes Played: ____

–   My strengths as a player in today's game:

–   My weaknesses as a player in today's game:

–   Team strengths (e.g., defense, offense, 5 v 6, 6 v 5) in today's game:

–   Team weaknesses in today's game:

–   Opponent's team strengths:

–   Opponent's team weaknesses:

- What was the "difference" in today's match:

- What team adjustment would you suggest for the next game against this opponent?

- Who was the Player of the Game and why?

- Other comments (e.g., team strategy, attitude, preparation....)

Player Check-in
Above Average (+)   Average (O)   Below Average (–)

Health   ____   *Nutrition:* Grains ____

Sleep   ____   Protein ____

Hydration ____   Veggies ____

Fitness   ____   Fruit   ____

Life Beyond Water Polo ____

Quotable Quote: _____

_____

Game Analysis I

Opponent: _____(Wins ___ Losses ___) Date: ____ Result:____

Location: ____ Record: Wins: ___ Losses: ___ Minutes Played: ____

– My strengths as a player in today's game:

– My weaknesses as a player in today's game:

– Team strengths (e.g., defense, offense, 5 v 6, 6 v 5) in today's game:

– Team weaknesses in today's game:

– Opponent's team strengths:

– Opponent's team weaknesses:

– What was the "difference" in today's match:

– What team adjustment would you suggest for the next game against this opponent?

– Who was the Player of the Game and why?

– Other comments (e.g., team strategy, attitude, preparation....)

Player Check-in
Above Average (+)   Average (O)   Below Average (–)

Health   ____

Sleep   ____

Hydration ____

Fitness   ____

Nutrition: Grains ____

Protein ____

Veggies ____

Fruit   ____

Life Beyond Water Polo ____

Quotable Quote: _____

_____

Game Analysis I

Opponent: _____(Wins ___ Losses ___) Date: ____ Result:____

Location: ____ Record: Wins: ___ Losses: ___ Minutes Played: ____

- My strengths as a player in today's game:

- My weaknesses as a player in today's game:

- Team strengths (e.g., defense, offense, 5 v 6, 6 v 5) in today's game:

- Team weaknesses in today's game:

- Opponent's team strengths:

- Opponent's team weaknesses:

– What was the "difference" in today's match:

– What team adjustment would you suggest for the next game against this opponent?

– Who was the Player of the Game and why?

– Other comments (e.g., team strategy, attitude, preparation....)

Player Check-in
Above Average (+)   Average (O)   Below Average (–)

Health   _____   *Nutrition:* Grains _____

Sleep   _____   Protein _____

Hydration _____   Veggies _____

Fitness   _____   Fruit   _____

Life Beyond Water Polo _____

Quotable Quote: _____

_____

Game Analysis II

Instructions for *Game Analyses II*

Throughout the water polo season, you'll have opportunities to analyze games that you've watched in person, on TV, or online. Filling out the *Game Analysis II* can help you look more objectively at those games. The *GAII* is a learning activity that will challenge you to watch a game more critically, more fully, and more like a coach than an athlete. Unpacking a water polo match with the *Game Analysis II* will guide you to becoming a more thoughtful *student of the game*.

-MODEL-

 *Game Analysis II*

Team #1: *Stanford*   Team #2: *UCLA*

Wins: *11*   Losses: *4*   Wins: *18*   Losses: *2*

Date: *November 23*   Location: *Avery Aquatic Center*

Strengths:

Defense in general
−5-man defense held UCLA scoreless on PP
−goalie play was exceptional
−2MD was fantastic
−great help/crash defense on set passes
−communication on defense

Execution on 6-man
−great post movement, rotation
−passing & movement to set up shots

Hustle, Energy, Focus
−chasing & recovering loose balls
−played with emotion & energy

Strengths:

Frontcourt offense
−worked ball well to 2M
−2M held position, recognized attack side
−patience when finding the right shot
−great drives and movement, quick

Defense
−goalie played well
−never let the game get out of hand

Dealing with adversity
−hostile road game
−came in top-ranked

Weaknesses:

Maintaining momentum
Unnecessary exclusions
−too aggressive pressing perimeter
−fouled too frequently, easy for UCLA to pass

Weaknesses:

Came out way too flat
5 on 6 defense
−shot blocking, near-side goals
6 on 5 offense
−poor passes
−2M slow in recovery to defense

Quarter Adjustments & Effects:

−Ball control in front court to avoid turnovers
−Smart drop on defense
−Use of shot clock to kill time

Quarter Adjustments & Effects:

−Not much success on adjustments w/ 6 on 5 plays
−Press Stanford's best shooters
−Drops on defense frontcourt

General Comments:

Centers

−strong, lengthy
−great swimmer defender
−endurance (played almost whole game)
−had huge goal
−great at gaining & holding position

Centers

−polished step out & finish
−held position well
−good finishing ability
−not great endurance
−slow recovering to defense
−liability on defense (drive def.)

Attackers/Drivers

−serious shooters (8,9,24) in drop zone
−post ups at 5 (10 and 2)
−good movement to free-up passes
−physical w/good speed
−occasional rushed shot
−suffocating press D

Attackers/Drivers

−fast and quick
−good, not great shooters
−good separation, timing on drives
−patient (don't force shots/passes)
−2M is primary option
−good drop press (not huge press)

Center Defenders

−good legs & swimming abilities
−worked well to avoid exclusion
−able to deflect balls passed into set

Center Defenders

−strong, big w/ good legs
−struggled to present position
−primary shooters in frontcourt offense
−hands up on set passes to allow
  crash D to come

Goalie

−had great game (11 saves)
−blocked a few point-blank shots
−good cage feel (no unnecessary tips)
−strong throughout the game
−good passer

Goalie

−small, explosive legs
−jumpy and can be out of position
−looks to help 2MD too much
−ignored the crowd

Players of the Game:

Stanford: Goalie, Attacker, 2MD
UCLA: Attacker, Goalie

Moment of the Game:

Our goalie Matt Cyr* blocks a point blank shot from UCLA late in the first half. UCLA's Murray received a kick-out pass from 2M and his defender had left him to help 2MD, giving Murray a clear lane to the goal. After a couple fakes, Murray tried to force one nearside and low past Cyr but was stuffed. Even though the game was still young and close at that point, this play set the tone for the game. The story of the game was not Stanford's offense, but their tough defense and this moment is a shining demonstration of the lockdown D. This block put life and energy not only in the entire Stanford team and coaches, but had the entire aquatic facility pumped up and energized. After seeing this play, I knew that there was no way Stanford was going to lose this game.

Final Analysis:

This is what a water polo game should look like. An 8-6 final score is the perfect balance between enough offense and exciting goals and good smart defense. A thriller from start to finish. Our goalie put himself on the map as one of, if not the best goalies in the country. UCLA came into game with only one loss and had just handed Stanford a huge 10-5 loss at the SoCal invitational the prior weekend. UCLA definitely expected a win in this game. For Stanford, this was a must win. After a disappointing finish in the SoCal invitational, Stanford needed this game to show the rest of MPSF that they are more than capable of knocking off a top team like UCLA. More than anything, this game showed that Stanford is a tough team mentality and have the character and maturity to forget about a tough tournament and focus on winning a big conference game. As expected, Stanford played very well in their home pool and established themselves as true title contenders. The game was televised adding to the excitement.

* Players' names have been changed.

Notes

Game Analysis II

Team #1_____ v. Team #2_____

Wins: ____ Losses: ____   Wins: ____ Losses: ____

Date: _____   Location: _____

Strengths: Strengths:

Weaknesses: Weaknesses:

Half-time adjustments & effects: Half-time adjustments & effects:

General Comments:

Centers   Centers

Attackers/Drivers   Attackers/Drivers

Center Defenders   Center Defenders

Goalie   Goalie

Players of the Game:

Moment of the Game:

Final Analysis:

Game Analysis II

Team #1_____ v. Team #2_____

Wins: ____ Losses: ____   Wins: ____ Losses: ____

Date: _____   Location: _____

Strengths: Strengths:

Weaknesses: Weaknesses:

Half-time adjustments & effects: Half-time adjustments & effects:

General Comments:

Centers   Centers

Attackers/Drivers   Attackers/Drivers

Center Defenders   Center Defenders

Goalie   Goalie

Players of the Game:

Moment of the Game:

Final Analysis:

 *Game Analysis II*

Team #1_____ v. Team #2_____

Wins: ____ Losses: ____   Wins: ____ Losses: ____

Date: _____   Location: _____

Strengths: Strengths:

Weaknesses: Weaknesses:

Half-time adjustments & effects: Half-time adjustments & effects:

General Comments:

Centers   Centers

Attackers/Drivers   Attackers/Drivers

Center Defenders   Center Defenders

Goalie   Goalie

Players of the Game:

Moment of the Game:

Final Analysis:

 *Game Analysis II*

Team #1_____ v. Team #2_____

Wins: ____ Losses: ____   Wins: ____ Losses: ____

Date: _____   Location: _____

Strengths: Strengths:

Weaknesses: Weaknesses:

Half-time adjustments & effects: Half-time adjustments & effects:

General Comments:

Centers   Centers

Attackers/Drivers   Attackers/Drivers

Center Defenders   Center Defenders

Goalie   Goalie

Players of the Game:

Moment of the Game:

Final Analysis:

 *Game Analysis II*

Team #1_____ v. Team #2_____

Wins: ____ Losses: ____   Wins: ____ Losses: ____

Date: _____   Location: _____

Strengths: Strengths:

Weaknesses: Weaknesses:

Half-time adjustments & effects: Half-time adjustments & effects:

General Comments:

Centers   Centers

Attackers/Drivers   Attackers/Drivers

Center Defenders   Center Defenders

Goalie   Goalie

Players of the Game:

Moment of the Game:

Final Analysis:

Performance Feedback

Instructions for *Performance Feedback* *

At different times throughout the season, your coach will ask you to fill out one of the following Performance Feedback forms immediately after a game. This form helps you look closely at the stress you experience before and during a game. As an athlete, writing about stressors can help you identify and manage those feelings in the future.

You'll also be asked to discuss your "self-talk." As you might guess, self-talk is the talking you do in your own head during a training session, a game, and everyday life. Often, self-talk happens without us even noticing. However, what you say to yourself before or during a game can impact the way that you feel and perform. Sports psychologists recognize the importance of positive self-talk in helping athletes achieve their potential.

*This Performance Feedback form is a modified version of one developed by Sheila Stawinski of the University of Vermont.

-MODEL-

Performance Feedback
Cliff Pandiscio, USA vs. Hungary*

Opponent: *Hungary* Date: *February 24*

What stressors did you experience before, during, and after this game?

A sense of being outmatched, yet needing to go in and give everything I had anyway.

How did you experience this stress? Did it manifest in your thoughts, in the way you felt, or in the way you acted?

Felt a little worn down, and maybe a little defeated. It had been a rough tournament so far.

Mark on this scale your level of excitement and motivation for the game.

0————————————— | ———5——————————————10
Too Low   Perfect   Too High

In a few words, describe your feelings at the various times in the day?

  Travel to game: *Stressed*

  Warm up: *Settled*

  Just before the game: *Determined*

  During the game: *Determined*

  After the game: *Disappointed with the loss, but satisfied with the score and my effort.*

What techniques did you use to manage any stress you experienced? How effective were you in controlling this stress?

Had to rise above. I got my mind and heart right, then I focused on my warm-up, and I got my mind set on simple things I would need to do in the game (visualizing, body movements, etc.).

How was your self-talk? Positive, negative, thoughtful?

Positive, but tried to get my mind off myself and focus on the game.

Describe how your stressors, excitement/motivation, and self-talk impacted your performance.

It got me ready for the game, and I gave my best performance of the tournament.

After unpacking your game-day mental state, what would you do differently to improve for the next game?

Focus on working with my teammates in my warm-up and not treating myself like an isolated segment. Prepare to work as a team, fighting with and for them.

Additional Thoughts: *None*

*Players' names have been changed.

Performance Feedback

Opponent: _____   Date: _____

What stressors did you experience before, during and after this game?

How did you experience this stress? Did it manifest in your thoughts, in the way you felt, or in the way you acted?

Mark on this scale your level of excitement and motivation for the game.

0———————————————————5———————————————————10
Too Low   Perfect   Too High

In a few words, describe your feelings at the various times in the day?

Travel to game:

Warm up:

Just before the game:

During the game:

After the game:

What techniques did you use to manage any stress you experienced? How effective were you in controlling this stress?

How was your self-talk? Positive, negative, thoughtful?

Describe how your stressors, excitement/motivation, and self-talk impacted your performance.

After unpacking your game-day mental state, what would you do differently to improve for the next game?

Additional Thoughts:

Performance Feedback

Opponent: _____   Date: _____

What stressors did you experience before, during and after this game?

How did you experience this stress? Did it manifest in your thoughts, in the way you felt, or in the way you acted?

Mark on this scale your level of excitement and motivation for the game.

0———————————————5———————————————10
Too Low   Perfect   Too High

In a few words, describe your feelings at the various times in the day?

Travel to game:

Warm up:

Just before the game:

During the game:

After the game:

What techniques did you use to manage any stress you experienced? How effective were you in controlling this stress?

How was your self-talk? Positive, negative, thoughtful?

Describe how your stressors, excitement/motivation, and self-talk impacted your performance.

After unpacking your game-day mental state, what would you do differently to improve for the next game?

Additional Thoughts:

Performance Feedback

Opponent: _____   Date: _____

What stressors did you experience before, during and after this game?

How did you experience this stress? Did it manifest in your thoughts, in the way you felt, or in the way you acted?

Mark on this scale your level of excitement and motivation for the game.

0 ⎯⎯⎯⎯⎯⎯⎯⎯⎯⎯⎯⎯ 5 ⎯⎯⎯⎯⎯⎯⎯⎯⎯⎯⎯⎯ 10
Too Low   Perfect   Too High

In a few words, describe your feelings at the various times in the day?

    Travel to game:

    Warm up:

    Just before the game:

    During the game:

    After the game:

What techniques did you use to manage any stress you experienced? How effective were you in controlling this stress?

How was your self-talk? Positive, negative, thoughtful?

Describe how your stressors, excitement/motivation, and self-talk impacted your performance.

After unpacking your game-day mental state, what would you do differently to improve for the next game?

Additional Thoughts:

Performance Feedback

Opponent: _____   Date: _____

What stressors did you experience before, during and after this game?

How did you experience this stress? Did it manifest in your thoughts, in the way you felt, or in the way you acted?

Mark on this scale your level of excitement and motivation for the game.

$$0\text{\textemdash\textemdash\textemdash\textemdash\textemdash}5\text{\textemdash\textemdash\textemdash\textemdash\textemdash}10$$
Too Low   Perfect   Too High

In a few words, describe your feelings at the various times in the day?

Travel to game:

Warm up:

Just before the game:

During the game:

After the game:

What techniques did you use to manage any stress you experienced? How effective were you in controlling this stress?

How was your self-talk? Positive, negative, thoughtful?

Describe how your stressors, excitement/motivation, and self-talk impacted your performance.

After unpacking your game-day mental state, what would you do differently to improve for the next game?

Additional Thoughts:

Performance Feedback

Opponent: _____   Date: _____

What stressors did you experience before, during and after this game?

How did you experience this stress? Did it manifest in your thoughts, in the way you felt, or in the way you acted?

Mark on this scale your level of excitement and motivation for the game.

0————————————5————————————10
Too Low   Perfect   Too High

In a few words, describe your feelings at the various times in the day?

Travel to game:

Warm up:

Just before the game:

During the game:

After the game:

What techniques did you use to manage any stress you experienced? How effective were you in controlling this stress?

How was your self-talk? Positive, negative, thoughtful?

Describe how your stressors, excitement/motivation, and self-talk impacted your performance.

After unpacking your game-day mental state, what would you do differently to improve for the next game?

Additional Thoughts:

Performance Feedback

Opponent: _____   Date: _____

What stressors did you experience before, during and after this game?

How did you experience this stress? Did it manifest in your thoughts, in the way you felt, or in the way you acted?

Mark on this scale your level of excitement and motivation for the game.

0⸺⸺⸺⸺⸺⸺5⸺⸺⸺⸺⸺⸺10
Too Low   Perfect   Too High

In a few words, describe your feelings at the various times in the day?

Travel to game:

Warm up:

Just before the game:

During the game:

After the game:

What techniques did you use to manage any stress you experienced? How effective were you in controlling this stress?

How was your self-talk? Positive, negative, thoughtful?

Describe how your stressors, excitement/motivation, and self-talk impacted your performance.

After unpacking your game-day mental state, what would you do differently to improve for the next game?

Additional Thoughts:

Performance Feedback

Opponent: _____   Date: _____

What stressors did you experience before, during and after this game?

How did you experience this stress? Did it manifest in your thoughts, in the way you felt, or in the way you acted?

Mark on this scale your level of excitement and motivation for the game.

```
0————————————5————————————10
Too Low          Perfect          Too High
```

In a few words, describe your feelings at the various times in the day?

Travel to game:

Warm up:

Just before the game:

During the game:

After the game:

What techniques did you use to manage any stress you experienced? How effective were you in controlling this stress?

How was your self-talk? Positive, negative, thoughtful?

Describe how your stressors, excitement/motivation, and self-talk impacted your performance.

After unpacking your game-day mental state, what would you do differently to improve for the next game?

Additional Thoughts:

Athletic Journals

"Keep a journal... This type of daily 'mental muscle' work will gradually improve your focus in practice and in games."

–Leif H. Smith & Todd M. Kays, sports psychologists

Writing an *Athletic Journal*

An Athlete's Journal provides you with a place to set goals, reflect, grapple with issues, keep track of training ideas, and record results as well as plan, scheme, ponder, rant, question, draw, and celebrate. The plain fact is that taking a few minutes to write amplifies your learning. These journal prompts will engage you and your teammates in different ways. And that difference is the beauty of such a learning activity.

Here are a few suggestions about writing responses to Athletic Journals.

- *Just Write It*. Don't be overly concerned with perfect writing. In other words, don't stop to check spelling, correct grammar, or create perfect paragraphs.

- *Quick Write*: When you're responding to the prompts in this section of your Team Notebook, try a Quick Write: write nonstop for 3 to 6 minutes. Do not take your pen or pencil off the paper. Keep writing. If your mind goes blank, make a list of words related to the topic until you start writing sentences again. Here's an example of a Quick Write by a player whose team lost to a lesser team. Notice the list of words in the middle that are in **bold typeface**:

> I don't like losing to a team we should have beaten. Last time this happened I felt empty inside and kind of sick. I think about the times I messed up during the game. I think about... **poor passes, times I didn't talk, moments when I lost focus, my emotions, referee decisions, teammates' mistakes, anger...** I know poor passes happen because sometimes I'm not calm. I've got to slow down my thinking. Same thing happens with my talk—I get too caught up in the moment of the game and forget to communicate to my teammates. It all comes down to my lack of focus when I let my emotions get the best of me. That's especially true when a referee makes a call I disagree with and I get angry and lose focus. I also get mad when a teammate messes up. I need to stay in the game—I need to slow things down in my mind.

- *Draw or sketch*. There are many ways to tell the story of your training and competing. Even if you can barely sketch stick figures, give drawing a try.

- *Word Web.* If you struggle to write one of the prompts in the following pages, try making a Word Web. Check out the example below in Figure 1. Place the writing prompt in the center of the page. Then, make a list of words that connect to the topic. Once you have 8-10 words, start writing about each word. You'll be surprised how your thoughts flow.

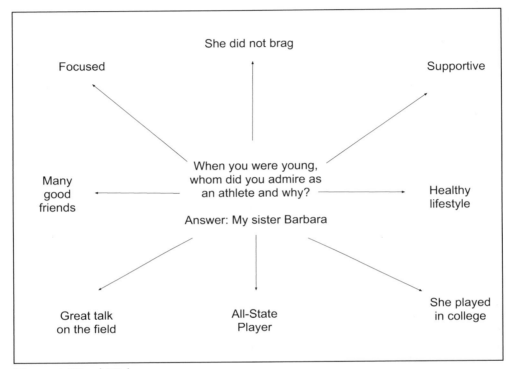

Figure 1 Word Web

- *This is your Notebook.* Remember, you have to approach the prompts on the following pages in your own way. Tell your truth and explore your own understanding of the questions, ideas, and situations presented.

Training

What makes training hard for you?

What makes training easy for you?

Your Timeline as a Water Polo Player

Create a timeline of your water polo career. Include your athletic milestones, important coaches, and various teams. Write above and below the timeline.

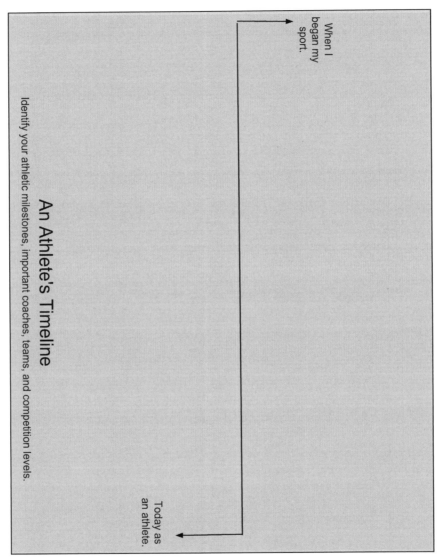

When I began my sport.

An Athlete's Timeline

Identify your athletic milestones, important coaches, teams, and competition levels.

Today as an athlete.

What's one thing you've noticed or thought about while filling out this timeline?

An Effective Coach

List up to five qualities of an effective coach:

1. _____

2. _____

3. _____

4. _____

5. _____

Tell the story of a good moment during a game or training session with one of your coaches:

The Perfect Warm-Up

Outline what you consider a perfect warm-up routine for a game. Include the approximate amount of time spent on each activity, and the reason you have included this activity.

Warm-up activity	Time	Why this activity?

Write about a favorite teammate or training partner.

Teammate's/Training Partner's Name_____

Qualities as an athlete:

Qualities as a person:

Unique habits or quirks:

Best story about this teammate:

What have you learned from this athlete?

Who brings out your best and why?

Who brings out the best in you as an athlete and why? You might first think of a coach or trainer. But also think about family members, fans, teammates, or even an opponent.

Making Meaning Activity: *Practice*

This writing activity will help you look more closely at your practices. You may also "make meaning" of other aspects of water polo like *wins, losses, teammates, opponents,* and *coaches.*

Step #1: List some of the words that come to mind when you think about "practice." Place the words in the chart below.

Step #2: Name the opposite of the words you've listed in Step One. Looking at both sides of any topic (i.e., true/false, positive/negative, right/wrong) can help us come to know a subject more fully.

Step #1 *Example: boring*	Step #2 *Example: exciting*

Step #3: Write two sentences about training using two pair of the opposing words from above. For example: "*Some days practice is* <u>boring</u> *because it's the same old same old; other days practice is* <u>exciting</u>, *because we're learning a next-level play and I know the team is growing.*"

Making Meaning Activity: *Practice* (cont.)

Step #4: Write a 5-sentence paragraph about <u>practice</u> using the guidelines below. This exercise will help you find your "truth" about training.

Sentence 1	a five-word statement
Sentence 2	a question
Sentence 3	two independent clauses combined by a semi-colon
Sentence 4	a sentence with an introductory phrase
Sentence 5	a two-word statement

Here's an example of a paragraph focused on a "training plan" written by US ski racer David Chamberlain:

"Training plans are sometimes stifling. When do they become this? On the days my body feels good the training plan seems fine; on days when my body feels bad I am scared that the training plan is too much for me. In July and November and sometimes the end of January, these are the months that I feel this the most. Must change."

Quick Response

Write a quick response and a reason for each:

My favorite training food is . . .

In water polo I get nervous about . . .

My favorite exercise or activity during a practice session is . . .

When our team wins a competition by a wide margin, I . . .

When my coach says _____ I feel like . . .

We Are Who We Spend the Most Time With

It's often said that we are who we spend the most time with. Who are the five people, athletes or not, that you spend the most time with? In what ways do they affect who you are as a person and as an athlete?

Injury or Illness

Let's say that you just tweaked your shoulder. What's the first thing you do? Who do you speak with? Think and write about how you organize yourself to get through an injury or illness.

Proudest Moment

Other than winning a game, tell the story of your proudest moment as a water polo player.

Photo Thoughts

In the space below paste a picture of yourself from a game or practice session. The photo could be from a newspaper clipping or Facebook.

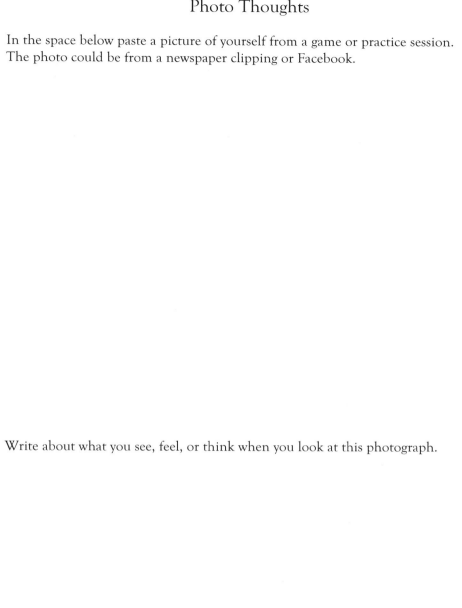

Write about what you see, feel, or think when you look at this photograph.

T-shirt Slogans

Come up with four t-shirt slogans/sayings about your team, water polo, competing, or training. Use the t-shirts provided.

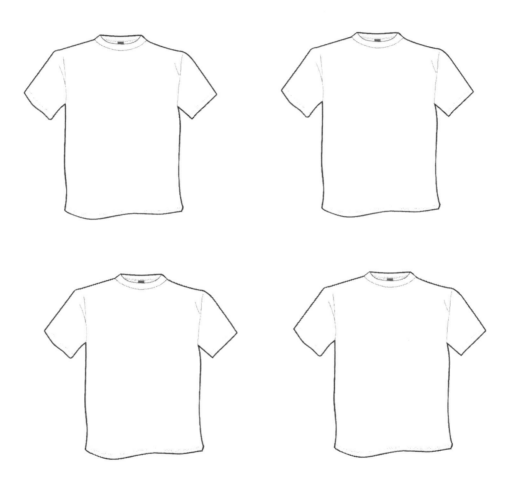

Advice or Talk

What advice or talk do you <u>least</u> like to hear before an important water polo game and why?

Failure

A class of sports psychology students explored how failure can be helpful. Among the list compiled by students were following—write about them:

Failure found what didn't work.

Failure creates hunger to do better.

Failure adds value to success.

Failure is feedback.

Michael Jordan on Success

Write about this quotation from basketball legend Michael Jordan:

"I've missed more than 9000 shots in my career. I've lost almost 300 games. 26 times, I've been trusted to take the game winning shot and missed. I've failed over and over and over again in my life. And that is why I succeed."

Quitting

Write about a time when you quit. It could have been while working on a math problem, washing dirty windows, or swimming sprints in practice. What leads you toward throwing in the towel and what makes you stop?

World-Class Thoughts

The following are themes written about in the journal of an elite, world-class athlete over the course of a year:

Loneliness	Relaxation	Lists
Training	Breathing	Equipment
Family	Preparation	Sponsors
Friends	Control	Balance
Focus	Routine	Alignment
Emotions	Yoga	Symmetry
Food	Writing	Asserting
Dreams	Need for	oneself
Body Tension	success	Satisfaction
Colors	Self-esteem	Optimism
Visualization	Playfulness	Goals
Awareness	Schedules	

First, what comes to mind when you read this list?

Second, select one of the themes. Write about the theme and how it relates to you as an athlete.

Performance Analysis

There are times just before a game that you feel "on." You're ready to have at it and everything is in sync. Some days... not so much. Why is that? What specific things affect your performance? Could it be friends, sleep, food, the opponent, your coach, or your mood? Make two lists—the good and the bad—of what may influence your performances in a game or practice session.

Good Performance	Bad Performance
Sample: I know my opponent.	Sample: I lack confidence

Write one or two sentences that capture your thinking about the lists above:

When you were young...

When you were young, whom did you admire as a player and why?

Writing a Game

In this entry you will tell "the story" of one of your games.

Game vs. _____ Date: _____

Describe the evening before this game. Discuss whether you prepared (e.g., rested) the way you should have. What might you have done differently?

How much sleep did you get the night before this game? Is this an optimal amount of sleep for you? What's your goal for sleep the night before a game?

On game day, how did you spend your time? What did you eat? Did you hydrate well? Did you exert energy unnecessarily? If you could improve upon one aspect of preparation for this game, what would that be?

Writing a Game (cont.)

Figure 1 below suggests ways that some players learn about their opponents. On the figure, circle the ways you learned about your opponent for this game. If you have other ways, add them to the figure.

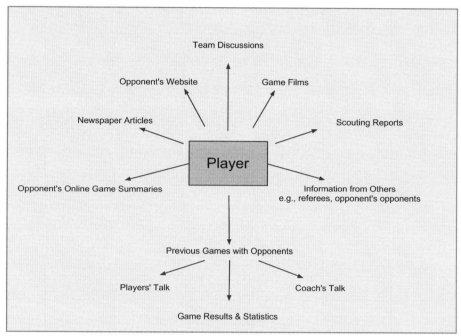

Figure 1, Ways Athletes Learn About an Opponent, Reprinted with Permission

Describe your pre-game "self talk." Were you confident or unsure? Did you visualize your play?

Writing a Game (cont.)

Describe your pre-game preparation (e.g., warm-up). What one aspect of your warm-ups would you improve upon?

Describe your awareness in the pool during the game. Did anything take your concentration away from the game? For example, did the opponents' fans draw your attention away from play or did you let other influences (e.g., an official's call, a coach's decision) trouble you?

Describe your post-game recovery (e.g., cool down). Did you stretch, hydrate, and eat appropriately? What one aspect of your post-game recovery would you improve upon?

Sum up your game in a six-word "story." Here's an example: "Yearlong training; offseason camps: Hat Trick!"

Coaches

Make a list of your coaches throughout your career. What do you think you learned from each one?

Coach	What I learned.

Instructional Water Polo Video

Think about one of the areas in water polo that you'd like to improve upon like a skill (e.g., shooting) or a tactic (e.g., moving to space). Find an instructional video on that topic to watch. You will be able to find many videos on Websites like YouTube. Respond to the following prompts:

Title of Video: _____

Where did you find it: _____

~Discuss the new information you learned from watching this video:

~What might you try out from this video:

~What questions did you have after watching the video:

~What ideas might you share with a teammate or friend:

~What knowledge might you share with your coach:

~What suggestions might you make for revising this video:

To a Teammate

Write a message to a teammate, past or present, with something about water polo that you'd like to share.

The Advantages of Playing Poorly

Why can this statement be true: "Some days, playing poorly is the most important result that could happen." Give examples from your own experiences as a water polo player.

Favorite Sports Movie

What's your favorite sports movie of all time and why? What do you like about the movie? Do you relate to anyone in the movie? Would you recommend this movie to a younger athlete? If so, why?

"It is more important to participate than to win."

—The Olympic Credo

Write about the Olympic Credo. Why do you think the Olympic Committee adopted this philosophy? Can you give any examples from your own athletic career when you witnessed or experienced this belief in action?

Top 10 List

Make a list of the top 10 things you admire about yourself as an athlete and person.

1.

2.

3.

4.

5.

6.

7.

8.

9.

10.

What's missing?

Look back at the list on the previous page. Write about what's missing.

Quick Response

Write about the following topics:

Mental preparedness for a game

Coping with anxiety or nervousness

Motivation

Managing Success

Handling a loss

How Do You Learn?

How do you learn your sport? Look at this figure and circle the ways you learn as an athlete.

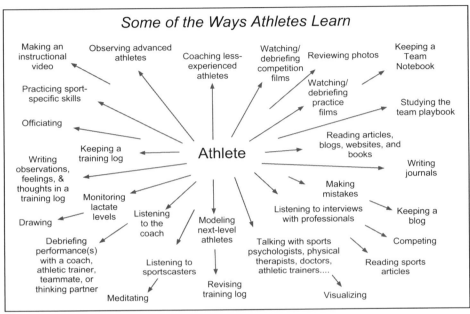

Reprinted with permission, *Writing on the Bus* (Kent, 2012, p. 14)

Looking at the various learning activities above, what could you add to your own experience to help you improve as an athlete?

Are there ways you learn that are not included in the figure above? List them below.

Are you getting enough sleep?

"Sleep is food for the brain."
                                                    –The National Sleep Foundation

Go back through your past week and add up the total hours of sleep you've had. Divide the total hours of sleep by the number of days.

___Total Hours of Sleep ÷ ___ Number of Days = ___ Average Nightly Hours

The National Sleep Foundation suggests that the average teenager needs 9 ¼ hours of sleep per night and the average child aged five to 12 needs 10-11 hours of sleep. Add an athlete's lifestyle to the equation and the hours of sleep necessary go up.

   –Write about your sleeping habits, especially during the water polo season:

Your Most Humiliating Day as an Athlete

Write about your most humiliating day as an athlete. After you've written about the experience, tell what you may have learned from it.

Stressed?

The American College of Sports Medicine listed the following signs and symptoms of stress in athletes.

Behavioral	Physical	Psychological
Difficulty sleeping	Feeling ill	Negative self-talk
Lack of focus, overwhelmed	Cold, clammy hands	Inability to concentrate
Consistently performs better in practice/training than in competition	Profuse sweating	Uncontrollable intrusive and negative thoughts or images
Substance abuse	Headaches	Self doubt
	Increased muscle tension	
	Altered appetite	

Referring to the chart above, write about your stress levels in each of the following areas:

Behavioral:

Physical:

Psychological:

Halftime Talk

Using a recent game, make up the halftime talk that you would have given as the opponent's coach. Remember to include as many specifics as possible. (This activity would be a good one for team members to share with one another.)

Your Choice

Select one or more of the terms on the left and write what comes to mind:

Poor sport

A good loss

Future star

Miscommunication

Injury

Suck-up

Cheap shots

Focus

Fitness

Teammate

Official

Coach

Trainer

Foul

Frightened

Poser

Discipline

Reward

Practice

Self Evaluation

At this moment in your career, what's your primary weakness as a water polo player? When asked to name a weakness, some athletes identified the following:

Unfit	Insecure	Unskilled	Uncommitted
Inexperienced	Unreliable	Unhealthy	Unfocused
Hot-tempered	Immature	Lazy	Disorganized
Know-it-all	Timid	Nervous	Inconsistent

What is your primary weakness _____.

Write about this weakness and then discuss your plans to improve.

Word Clouds

Go back through your completed journal entries and *Game Analyses I & II*. Select individual words that reflect you and your season thus far. Using a free online Word Cloud program like Wordle (www.wordle.net) or Tagxedo (www.tagxedo.com), create a word-art interpretation of your sports season so far. Print the Word Cloud, trim it, and tape it over the model supplied below. If you don't have access to Internet, sketch your own Word Cloud.

Mental Imagery: Creating Personal and Team Highlight Reels

Think back to your best moments as a player. Remember the details of that perfect pass or powerful attack that helped produce a goal. Perhaps you shut down the other team's leading scorer. Now, make a list of those moments and create your own mental video that you can play back to yourself to prepare for a game or use during a game to gain back confidence.

Instant Highlight Reel (10 to 30 seconds – all you as a player):

Do the same but include team moments such as stringing a half-dozen passes together that end in a goal or an overtime win against a higher-seeded team.

Highlight Reel (2 to 5 minutes – personal and as a team):

Songs of My Sport

Make a list of your favorite songs:

Which favorite songs would you play...

The night before an important game:
Song title: _____

Practice:
Song title: _____

The morning of a game:
Song title: _____

During a game:
Song title: _____

After an upset win:
Song title: _____

After a loss to an opponent you could have beaten:
Song title: _____

When the season ends:
Song title: _____

Others times: _____
Song title: _____

Others times: _____
Song title: _____

Your Thoughtful Side

Write about the kindest thing you have ever done as an athlete.

Draw Water Polo

Draw whatever comes to mind when you think of water polo. It could be a piece of equipment, a place, a teammate, an OT win, the taste of chlorine... Write a title and caption for your drawing.

Title _____

Caption _____

_____

Good Words

What positive story would you like told about a teammate, coach, fan, or opponent?

The Benefits of Journal Writing

Dr. Stephanie Dowrick identifies the following benefits of journaling:

- reduces stress and anxiety
- increases self-awareness
- sharpens mental skills
- promotes genuine psychological insight
- advances creative inspiration and insight
- strengthens coping abilities

As an athlete who has been keeping a team notebook, have you experienced any of these benefits? Explain.

Slow Down the Game

The game of water polo is fast paced and has many decisions. A player's head can be full of clutter (e.g., information from other players, from a coach, fan noise). To slow down the game, refocus, and manage anxiety, many athletes use centering breaths.

Centering Breaths:

- Take a deep breath from your abdomen and feel your neck and shoulder muscles relax as you inhale.
- Inhale for about 6 seconds and exhale slowly for about 8-10 seconds.

Activity:

Write about a time in a game that your head was full of clutter or you were anxious. Go back to that time in your mind and practice using the centering breaths to slow down the game and release the clutter so you can make quicker and spot on decisions. As you exhale slowly, start to focus on a positive aspect of your play. Keep it simple and use your visual senses to bring this positive picture to life.

Words of the Game

Watch a competition on television, video, or online. Make a list of the best lines spoken by the commentators, coaches, or athletes.

Sports Psychology

All professional teams and some collegiate teams have the support of sport psychologists. Their work involves helping athletes with issues like the following:

Mental preparedness   Goal setting

Managing Anxiety   Reward strategies

Coping with Success   Visualization

Handling Failure   Motivation

If you're not familiar with some of these terms, do a quick online search. Now, page back through your reflections, game analyses, and journals and think how your writing in this notebook has helped you with any of these concerns. Write...

Moments of the Season

Throughout a water polo season you experience highs and lows, ups and down. Think back through the season and give quick examples of the following:

I laughed...

I got emotional...

I screamed like a wild person...

I got crazy angry...

I sat and stared in disbelief...

I just didn't care...

I wanted to go hide...

I wanted someone to see...

Your Water Polo Season

Think about your water polo season and draw whatever comes to mind.

Retrospective

Go back through the words you've written in this team notebook and make a list below and on the next page of your sentences, phrases, and words that are interesting, fun, introspective, and quirky about your season thus far.

Additional Journal Prompts

1. *The Natural*: If you're a natural athlete, describe what it's like to someone who is not. If you're not a natural athlete, write about what it's like to train with or compete against someone who is. If you are a natural athlete, what's your biggest frustration. If you are not, why has that been a good thing for you?

2. List ten of your favorite all-time quotations by players and coaches from your experiences or from those you've heard about.

3. Tell about a time when you were genuinely happy for another athlete's poor performance or loss. How does that make you feel now?

4. Describe your greatest disappointment as an athlete thus far in your career. What did you learn from the experience?

5. Who's the oldest water polo player you know. Describe the player. What characteristics of the player do you admire?

6. Describe your earliest memory as a water polo player.

7. If you could relive one moment as a player, what would it be and why would you want to go back?

8. "Champions aren't made in the gyms. Champions are made from something they have deep inside them ~ a desire, a dream, a vision." Write about this quotation from the great heavyweight boxer Muhammad Ali.

9. Describe the best competition in any sport that you've seen in person as a fan.

10. Have you ever been dishonest as an athlete? If so, why? What did you learn from this experience? If you haven't been dishonest or don't want to write about it, have you witnessed dishonesty on the part of another athlete? If so, how did it make you feel?

11. At the present moment what three non-athletic jobs look as if they might give you the same "feeling" that competitive athletics do? Explain your thinking.

12. Where do you see yourself in the next few years as an athlete?

13. What is something you dislike about yourself as an athlete?

14. Think back to a time when an athlete you knew or admired bombed big-time in an event that he or she was favored to win. Describe your feelings.

15. What is your favorite place to compete and why?

16. Write about a frustrating experience you've had as an athlete.

17. When is training an absolute joy?

18. Under what circumstances would you allow a competitor to beat you on purpose.

19. What books would you recommend to a young athlete?

20. Look back at the results of the last competition you won or did well in. Think about the losing team. Write about the game from the perspective of a player on the losing team.

21. Write from the perspective of the top athlete in your sport using any of these prompts—

> "When I win a competition by a wide margin, I..."
> "My worst performance in the past six months made me feel..."
> "When other athletes talk about me they say..."
> "I am frightened about..."

22. Tape your favorite newspaper article about your season in the Notes section of this workbook. If you or your team didn't make the newspapers, print and include a favorite Facebook or blog post. Write about what has been written.

23. Write about the following quotation by alpine ski racer Carter Robinson: "No one likes skiing with a cluttered mind, so put it on paper and free some space."

24. Create a crossword puzzle of water polo or your team with a free online program like Puzzle-Maker.com

25. Found Poem: Honest... the following activity is fun and helps athletes see a game more fully by thinking more deeply. Here are the steps toward creating a Found Poem:

- Find a newspaper article written about you, your team, or another athlete/team that you admire;

- Read the article and underline words, phrases, or lines that you like or find interesting. Put those words into a non-rhyming poem that tells a story.

- Here are the opening lines from an article by Barry Faulkner (*Dailey Pilot*, 2/5/10) about the Sea Kings' captain, Victoria Kent. We've highlighted our favorite words and phrases that might be used in a poem. We have not included the entire article.

CORONA del MAR'S LIFEBLOOD

NEWPORT BEACH —If actions speak louder than words, how one acts in a pool of their own blood speaks to the soul of any competitor.

And Victoria Kent's actions after being cracked in the mouth hard enough to require 15 stitches Saturday, said a mouthful about the Corona del Mar High girls' water polo standout....

We added a few of our own words to create a Found Poem:

LIFEBLOOD

Actions do speak louder than words.
But for the captain,
It's just another day in the pool:
Fifteen stitches and
A mouthful of blood for the
Sea Kings' senior machine.
And now, with
Blue sutures for
The winter formal,
("They match my dress")
She dives back into the pool with
Resilience and her teammates,
Displaying, as always,
The soul of a competitor.

26. If I were not competing in my sport, I would be _____ because _____. Explain.

27. *What was I thinking?* Go back through your journal and log and pick out the comical, nonsensical, and mindless lines you've written and write them below. Enjoy...

28. Write a conversation between you and an incredibly gifted young athlete who is not living up to her or his potential.

29. What's your earliest memory of a bitter loss?

27. Video Comments: If your team has video taken of games, write a paragraph summarizing a competition as if you were the team's public relations person or a sports caster summarizing the game for television.

28. If appropriate, trade notebooks with a teammate or friend and write an observation of the athlete with respect to training, competition, or life beyond athletics.

29. Draw a picture of a particular moment from the season.

30. As someone who is keeping a journal, how do you feel about this quotation by Grace Paley: "We write about what we don't know about what we know."

31. Write about this quotation from Boston Marathon winner Amby Burfoot: "To get to the finish line, you'll have to try lots of different paths."

32. Think back to the teams you've been on: what phrase or term was used a lot on each team?

33. Pre-game study: Answer the following about the opponent you are about to face:

> -If you have played this opponent before, what do you remember about the last game?
> -What have reliable sources said about the opponents' strengths/weaknesses?
> -What's one strategy or approach that you or your team should try against this opponent?
> -What's your overall game plan?

34. Practicing to the Next Level: Write about a recent practice session. What could you have done differently to move toward the next level?

35. What is a good opponent?

36. After a competition you participated in, write a performance analysis of a teammate or fellow athlete.

Team-Building Activities

Team-Building Activities

During different times of the season, your coach will divide the team into small groups of 2-4 athletes. Each group will discuss and come to an agreement on the responses for the following activities. Some times your group's responses will be shared with the entire team; other times, the discussions and results will remain among the group members. If your coach chooses not to use these activities, you may complete most of these on your own or with teammates as optional Athletic Journal entries.

Tag a Teammate

Under each category, name a teammate. Give an example or two of the athlete's qualities.

Tag a Teammate

Who'd make a great coach?	A true sportsman	Dedication plus	Kindest
Most coachable	Always leaves it on the field	Most motivating	Great future
Great opponent	Team Leader	Fun	Positive
Healthy	Student-Athlete: the complete package	Who should take the last shot	Fitness Fanatic

Create a *New* Play

Create a new play to introduce to the team and coaching staff.

So far this season...

The funniest thing we've witnessed...

The happiest we've been...

The thing we thought but did not say to a coach, opponent, official, or teammate...

The moment we wish we could relive as a team...

What are the various reasons you play water polo?

All-Star Team

Your coach will divide you up into small groups and ask you to think about the players in your district, conference, or state. In your small groups, discuss who you would select for your all-star team. Select 6 players and a goalie plus 3 alternates. Write your choices on chart paper in team formation. Each group will hang up their chart paper. Staying in your group, go from chart to chart and compare your choices with your teammates' selections. After reviewing all of the charts, feel free to go back and revise your all-star team. Your coaches can end this activity by having you discuss and vote on an all-star team from your district, conference, or state.

Team History & Trivia

Over the course of several days, seek out as much of your team's history and trivia as possible. Your group will look at traditional water polo records as well as the unconventional. Here is a small list to jumpstart your group's thinking:

Top Goal Scorer

Top Assist Leader

Top Goalkeeper

Overall team records

Championships

Farthest Traveled

Coaches

Assistant Coaches

All-Conference

All-League

All-State players

Uniforms photos

What We Think About...

What we think about during training.

What we think about during a game.

What we think about after a win.

What we think about after a loss.

At This Moment...

Write about the following as they pertain to your group at this point in the season.

Training

Games

Coaching

Sleep/Rest

Nutrition

Travel to away games

Life beyond sport (e.g., family, school, work)

The rest of the season

What we need right now

The Season's Stats

Come up with as many statistics as possible from your competitive season thus far. These stats may be serious or not. Some figures will be estimated. Here are a few ideas to jumpstart your list—you may want to use a Notes Pages at the back of your notebook to complete the list:

-How many training hours?

-Number of miles traveled to games?

-How many games?

-How many hours/yards swum?

-Stats about scores, wins, and losses.

-How many hours lifting weights?

How many bananas eaten? Pizzas?

-How often did you stop at fast-food place after a competition or practice?

More:

This Season

In your small group discuss what are you going to miss about this season?

Injury Rehabilitation Plan

Instructions for Injury Rehabilitation Plan

Part of playing water polo can include getting injured. How you manage your rehabilitation has a great deal to do with how quickly you'll be back in the pool. Sit with your athletic trainer, doctor, or coach to fill out the Injury Rehabilitation Plan. Your trainer or doctor may use a different form. Understanding your plan and staying organized will get you back into the game sooner.

-MODEL-

Injury Rehabilitation Plan

Injury Date: *Tuesday, July 18*   Trainer: *Aaron P.*

Diagnosis: *moderate knee sprain*

Projected Timeline to Recovery: *5-7 days . . . approximately.*

Rehabilitation Plan:

Tuesday: RICE (Rest, Ice, Compression and Elevation). ACE bandage or brace. Check with parents about using anti-inflammatory medications for pain relief.
Wednesday: keep elevated when seated. See me in the afternoon.

Training Plan while Injured:

Wednesday: depending on severity use the weight room and swimming pool. Ice therapy w/ me.
Thursday: RICE, keep elevated in school, see me . . . pool?
Friday: keep elevated, RICE, see me, pool.
Saturday: TBA . . . see me on Friday

What can you do to improve an aspect of your play while rehabilitating?

Swimming for upper body. Watch game videos. Stay connected with teammates by rehabbing on pool deck.

What can you do for your teammates and coaches while rehabilitating?

   –Don't whine about the injury.
   –Stay positive about recovery.

Other thoughts:

Keep your mind in the game!

Injury Rehabilitation Plan

Injury Date:

Diagnosis:

Projected Timeline to Recovery:

Rehabilitation Plan:

Training Plan while Injured:

What can you do to improve an aspect of your play while rehabilitating?

What can you do for your teammates and coaches while rehabilitating?

Other thoughts:

Injury Rehabilitation Plan

Injury Date:

Diagnosis:

Projected Timeline to Recovery:

Rehabilitation Plan:

Training Plan while Injured:

What can you do to improve an aspect of your play while rehabilitating?

What can you do for your teammates and coaches while rehabilitating?

Other thoughts:

Injury Rehabilitation Plan

Injury Date:

Diagnosis:

Projected Timeline to Recovery:

Rehabilitation Plan:

Training Plan while Injured:

What can you do to improve an aspect of your play while rehabilitating?

What can you do for your teammates and coaches while rehabilitating?

Other thoughts:

Notes Pages

"We write about what we don't know about what we know."

—Grace Paley

Date_____   Title_____

Date_____ Title_____

Notes

Date_____   Title_____

Date_____   Title_____

Notes

Date_____   Title_____

Date_____   Title_____

Notes

Date_____   Title_____

Date_____   Title_____

Notes

Date_____   Title_____

Date_____   Title_____

Notes

Date_____   Title_____

209

Date_____   Title_____

Notes

Date_____   Title_____

Date_____   Title_____

Notes

Date_____   Title_____

Date_____ Title_____

Notes

Date_____   Title_____

Date_____   Title_____

Notes

Date_____   Title_____

Date_____   Title_____

Notes

Date_____   Title_____

Date_____   Title_____

Notes

Coach's Comments

"A good coach will make players see what they can be rather than what they are."

—Ara Parseghian

Coach's Comments   Date_____

Coach's Comments   Date_____

Coach's Comments   Date_____

Coach's Comments   Date_____

About the Authors

Richard Kent

John Vargas

Richard Kent is a professor at the University of Maine and the director emeritus of the Maine Writing Project, a site of the National Writing Project. He is the author of many books, including *Writing on the Bus*, *The Athlete's Workbook*, and *VO₂ Max Athlete's Journal*, and maintains a resource website at WritingAthletes.com. An athletic coach for over 35 years, Kent is the proud uncle of three water polo players: Tyler, Ryan, and Victoria Kent. Most days, he can be found hiking, running, or cross-country skiing the mountains of western Maine with his Bernese Mountain Dog, Bailey Tuckerman.

John Vargas has enjoyed a distinguished water polo career as a player and coach for over 35 years. A two-time All-American and 1982 national champion as a player at UC Irvine, Vargas went on to a 10-year playing career with the USA Water Polo Senior National Team which included a fourth-place finish at the 1992 Olympic Games in Barcelona. He joined the national team coaching staff in 1993, serving as an assistant coach for the U.S. at the 1996 Atlanta Games; he served as head coach from 1997-2000, guiding the team at the 2000 Olympics in Sydney. He coached for 19 years at Corona del Mar High School in Newport Beach (CA) before moving on to head coach of Stanford men's water polo, where he has won an NCAA title (2002). In 2014, Vargas begins his 13th season with the Cardinal.

Write. Learn. Perform.

10937589R00129

Made in the USA
San Bernardino, CA
02 May 2014